JAN 2010

Animal Attack and Defense

TRICKY BEHAVIOR

Kimberley Jane Pryor

Marshall Cavendish
Benchmark

New York

First published in 2008 by
MACMILLAN EDUCATION AUSTRALIA PTY LTD
15–19 Claremont Street, South Yarra 3141

Visit our website at www.macmillan.com.au or go directly to www.macmillanlibrary.com.au

Associated companies and representatives throughout the world.

Copyright © Kimberley Jane Pryor 2009

Library of Congress Cataloging-in-Publication Data

Pryor, Kimberley Jane.
   Tricky behavior / by Kimberley Jane Pryor.
        p. cm. – (Animal attack and defense)
   Includes index.
   Summary: "Discusses how animals use tricky behavior to protect themselves from predators or to catch prey"–
   Provided by publisher.
   ISBN 978-0-7614-4425-1
   1. Animal defenses–Juvenile literature. I. Title.
   QL759.P793 2009
591.47–dc22

                                                                        2009004993

Edited by Julia Carlomagno
Text and cover design by Ben Galpin
Page layout by Domenic Lauricella
Photo research by Claire Armstrong and Legend Images

Printed in the United States

Acknowledgments
The author and the publisher are grateful to the following for permission to reproduce copyright material:

Cover and title page photo of a queen parrotfish in a protective sac © Getty Images/David Doubilet/National
Geographic

Photos courtesy of: © AfriPics.com/Alamy/Photolibrary, **28**; © Arco Images GmbH/Alamy/Photolibrary, **20**; ©
Blickwinkel/Alamy/Photolibrary, **18**; © Mike Gillam/Auscape, **30** (right); © Robert Shantz/Alamy/Photolibrary, **12**;
© Doug Perrine/Seapics.com/Auscape, **6**; © Johnbell/Dreamstime.com, **17**; © Ryszard Laskowski/Dreamstime.
com, **21**; © Ian Scott/Dreamstime.com, **30 (left)**; © Getty Images/Fred Bavendam, **27**; © Getty Images/David
Doubilet/National Geographic, **19**; © Getty Images/George Grall, **29**; © Getty Images/Frans Lemmens, **4**; © Getty
Images/Jim Merli, **15**; © Getty Images/Purestock, **22**; © Getty Images/Gail Shumway, **16**; © Flavia Bottazzini/
iStockphoto.com, **9**; © Eric Naud/iStockphoto.com, **13**; © Mark Papas/iStockphoto.com, **8**; Photolibrary/Tim
Davis, **7**; Photolibrary/Gilbert S Grant, **26**; Photolibrary/Zigmund Leszczynski, **23**, **24**; Photolibrary/Raymond
Mendez, **5**; Photolibrary/R Andrew Odum, **25**; Photolibrary/David M Schleser, **14**; Photolibrary/James Zipp, **10**;
Wikimedia Commons/Dezidor, **11**.

While every care has been taken to trace and acknowledge copyright, the publisher tenders their apologies for
any accidental infringement where copyright has proved untraceable. Where the attempt has been unsuccessful,
the publisher welcomes information that would redress the situation.

For Nick, Ashley, and Thomas

1 3 5 6 4 2

Contents

Glossary Word

When a word is printed in **bold**, you can look up its meaning in the glossary on page 31.

Types of Tricky Behavior

Animals use all types of tricky behavior to defend themselves from **predators**. Some animals live in groups, so there are many eyes to watch for danger. Animals that live alone need to have a few tricks to outwit predators. Some of these animals play dead or swell up. Some animals produce disgusting smells, or worse!

To protect their young, southern giant petrels can shoot disgusting vomit at intruders.

How Tricky Behavior Protects Animals

Tricky behavior gives animals a better chance of escaping from predators in their **habitats**.

Animals have to act quickly when they are attacked. If they do not do something amazing, they may become **prey** for hungry predators. Clever tricks and scary surprises confuse and frighten predators. Tricky behaviors like these give animals time to make speedy getaways.

The Texas horned lizard squirts blood from its eyes when it is attacked.

Schooling Fish

A huge school of fish is an awesome sight. There are so many fish that predators become confused by the color and movement.

Fish live in schools to lower their chances of getting caught and eaten by predators. When a school of fish is under attack, it becomes a dense, swirling ball of glittery fish. Predators find it almost impossible to keep sight of, and catch, a single fish.

Vital Statistics

- **Size:** less than 0.4 inches to about 8.2 feet (1 centimeter to 2.5 meters)
- **Habitat:** ponds, rivers, and oceans
- **Distribution:** fresh and saltwaters worldwide
- **Predators:** other fish, dolphins, whales, sharks, and seabirds

A School of Fish

A single school of herrings, sardines, or anchovies can have millions, or even billions, of fish.

Schooling fish form dense, swirling balls which make it hard for predators to pick out a single fish.

Adélie penguins gather together in groups before diving into the water.

Penguins

Diving into the ocean to catch a meal is a risky business for penguins. Predators such as leopard seals lurk in the freezing water.

Penguins dive into the water in groups to reduce the risk of one penguin being seized by a predator. When penguins are hungry, they waddle and slide to the water's edge and check for predators. Then they check again, and again. Finally they all rush to the edge and dive headlong into the water.

Vital Statistics

- **Height:** 1.1 to 3.8 ft (35 cm to 1.15 m)
- **Habitat:** cold southern seas and islands
- **Distribution:** Antarctica and subantarctic islands
- **Predators:** leopard seals and whales

A Penguin Rookery

Penguins usually breed in huge colonies, called rookeries. A rookery often contains hundreds of thousands of penguins.

Vital Statistics

- **Standing height:** 1 ft (30 cm)
- **Habitat:** Kalahari Desert
- **Distribution:** Africa
- **Predators:** eagles, hawks, and jackals

Meerkats

Meerkats help other meerkats to stay out of danger. At least one meerkat watches for predators while the others play or search for food.

Meerkats live in groups, and they depend on one another for survival. One meerkat usually stands guard for the group while the others scratch in the sand for insects. The guard gives an alarm call to warn the others if a predator approaches. Then the whole group dashes to the safety of the burrow.

A Meerkat Keeping Watch

A meerkat stands on a mound of sand or climbs a tree to watch for danger. Both males and females keep watch.

An adult meerkat stands guard to warn its family if danger is nearby.

Some sulphur-crested cockatoos always keep watch while the rest of the flock is feeding.

Sulphur-Crested Cockatoos

Sulphur-crested cockatoos live in **flocks**. A few sulphur-crested cockatoos keep watch each time the flock feeds.

Sulphur-crested cockatoos feed on the ground. They spend the morning and the late afternoon scratching around for seeds. A few birds perch in the trees to look for danger. These birds give loud screeches if they spot a predator, and the whole flock flies away.

Vital Statistics

- **Length:** 1.6 ft (49 cm)
- **Habitat:** forests and farmlands
- **Distribution:** Australia
- **Predators:** birds of prey

A Sulphur-Crested Cockatoo Keeping Watch

A sulphur-crested cockatoo keeping watch perches at the top of a tree. It **scans** the area for predators, such as falcons.

Gulls form a mob and squawk and fly at bigger birds to scare them away.

Vital Statistics

- **Length:** 11.4 in to 2.5 ft (29 to 76 cm)
- **Habitat:** swamps, lakes, and coasts
- **Distribution:** every continent except Antarctica
- **Predators:** crows, eagles, and foxes

A Gull's Mobbing Behavior

Gulls mob predators because a group can force a predator to leave more easily than a single bird can.

Gulls

Most gulls defend themselves and their chicks by mobbing predators. They gang up on predators until they drive them away.

Gulls help each other to defend their nests against predators. When a gull sees a predator, it makes loud alarm calls and flies at the predator. Other gulls hear the alarm calls and quickly join in. They all squawk and fly around the predator until it moves on.

Southern Cassowaries

Southern cassowaries are the world's most dangerous birds. They can cause serious, or even deadly, injuries.

Southern cassowaries can rip apart predators, such as dogs. They lash out with their powerful legs and feet when threatened or cornered. They can even injure or kill humans.

Vital Statistics

- **Height:** 4.9 to 6.6 ft (1.5 to 2 m)
- **Habitat:** rain forests
- **Distribution:** Australia and New Guinea
- **Predators:** dogs

A Southern Cassowary's Feet

Each of the southern cassowary's feet has three toes with strong claws. The claw on the inner toe is a long, dagger-like spike:

A southern cassowary has powerful feet and enormous claws to kick predators.

Desert Cottontails

A Desert Cottontail's Freezing Behavior

A desert cottontail crouches low and stays still, so that it seems to disappear into its surroundings.

Desert cottontails freeze rather than run when they sense danger. They stay completely still, hoping that they will not be seen.

A desert cottontail freezes to trick predators that **rely** on their sense of sight to find prey. When a desert cottontail sees a predator, it stays still so that its movements do not attract attention. Then, if it thinks it has time to escape, it hops away in a zigzag pattern.

A desert cottontail freezes and tries to blend in with its surroundings when threatened by a predator.

Staying still helps them to escape a predator's attention.

Duikers freeze or dive for cover when they sense danger.

Vital Statistics

- **Height at shoulder:** up to 2.1 ft (64 cm)
- **Habitat:** forests and dense bushlands
- **Distribution:** Africa
- **Predators:** snakes, eagles, jackals, and leopards

Duikers

Duikers are rarely seen by predators because of their freezing behavior. They crouch down and freeze to avoid detection.

Duikers rely on freezing behavior to keep themselves safe. They stand completely still at the slightest sign of danger. If duikers are approached, they dash away into the safety of thick bushes.

A Duiker's Freezing Behavior

When a duiker senses danger, it freezes immediately. It does not move any part of its body until the danger has passed, or it decides to dive for cover.

13

A Virginia opossum can "play 'possum" for up to four hours.

Vital Statistics

- **Length with tail:** 3.3 ft (1 m)
- **Habitat:** trees
- **Distribution:** North, Central, and South America
- **Predators:** hawks, owls, foxes, and coyotes

A Virginia Opossum Playing Dead

When a Virginia opossum plays dead, it drools and lets its tongue flop out of its mouth.

Virginia Opossums

Virginia opossums play dead when they feel threatened. This tricky behavior is also called "playing 'possum."

When a Virginia opossum is faced with danger, it falls to the ground and pretends to be dead. It lies very still, breathes slowly and shallowly, and doesn't blink its eyes at all. A Virginia opossum also leaks a smelly green liquid from its bottom to make itself even less appealing!

Eastern Hog-nosed Snakes

Vital Statistics

- **Length:** 1.6 to 3.8 ft (50 cm to 1.15 m)
- **Habitat:** open, sandy woodlands
- **Distribution:** North America
- **Predators:** larger snakes and birds of prey

Eastern hog-nosed snakes **deter** predators by playing dead. They even make themselves smell rotten.

An eastern hog-nosed snake flattens its head and neck when threatened. It hisses and lunges at predators, but rarely bites them. If hissing at a predator does not work, an eastern hog-nosed snake will **writhe** about and spread feces and a foul-smelling substance on itself. It sometimes vomits as well. Finally, it rolls onto its back and pretends to be dead.

An Eastern Hog-nosed Snake Playing Dead

An eastern hog-nosed snake plays dead with its mouth open and its forked tongue hanging out.

An eastern hog-nosed snake lies belly-up when it plays dead.

Scary Colors and Sounds ...

A red-eyed tree frog flashes its blue and white colors to startle predators as it escapes.

Vital Statistics

- **Length:** 0.4 in to 1 ft (1 to 30 cm)
- **Habitat:** rain forests, other forests, and deserts
- **Distribution:** every continent except Antarctica
- **Predators:** fish, turtles, crocodiles, lizards, snakes, and birds

A Frog's Flash Colors

A frog's flash colors are bright colors, such as red, orange, yellow, or blue. Flash colors sometimes form patterns of spots or stripes.

Frogs

Some frogs have bright colors on their sides, bellies, or back legs. These colors flash out as they leap away from predators.

Some frogs have hidden colors that they use to scare predators. When a predator attacks a frog, the frog leaps for safety and its bright colors are suddenly **revealed**. These colors surprise and confuse the predator, and this gives the frog time to escape.

Rattlesnakes

The sound of a rattlesnake's rattle is a warning that victims who survive remember for a long time.

A rattlesnake usually slithers off into the bushes if disturbed. However, if it feels cornered, a rattlesnake shakes the rattle on the tip of its tail to warn predators to move away. Predators that ignore the warning are given a deadly **venomous** bite.

Vital Statistics

- **Length:** 1 to 8.2 ft (30 cm to 2.5 m)
- **Habitat:** arid regions
- **Distribution:** North, Central, and South America
- **Predators:** eagles and hawks

A Rattlesnake's Rattle

A rattlesnake's rattle is made up of loosely connected parts. The parts bump against each other to make the buzzing sound.

The rattle on the tip of a rattlesnake's tail is used to scare predators away.

California ground squirrels mask their own scent with rattlesnake scent.

Vital Statistics

- **Length with tail:** about 1.5 ft (45 cm)
- **Habitat:** woodlands and grasslands
- **Distribution:** North America
- **Predators:** rattlesnakes, eagles, raccoons, coyotes, foxes, badgers, and weasels

A California Ground Squirrel's Scent

A California ground squirrel also masks its natural scent with rattlesnake scent taken from soil and other surfaces.

California Ground Squirrels

California ground squirrels make themselves smell like their archenemies: rattlesnakes!

California ground squirrels munch on the skins **shed** by rattlesnakes. Then they lick their fur to spread the rattlesnake scent. The rattlesnake scent masks the squirrel scent. At night, when squirrels are sleeping, passing predators smell rattlesnake and leave the squirrels alone.

Parrotfish

Some parrotfish sleep in a mucus "sleeping bag" at night. The mucus helps to mask their scent from hungry night feeders.

Some parrotfish trick predators that rely on their sense of smell to find prey. As night falls, parrotfish tuck themselves into crevices in a coral reef. Each parrotfish releases a cloud of mucus, which surrounds and protects it. This mucus masks the parrotfish's scent, so it is harder for predators to find.

Vital Statistics

- **Length:** up to 4.3 ft (1.3 m)
- **Habitat:** coral reefs
- **Distribution:** Atlantic, Indian, and Pacific oceans and the Red Sea
- **Predators:** moray eels and sharks

A Parrotfish's Scent

A parrotfish that makes a mucus "sleeping bag" is less likely to be eaten by a predator than a parrotfish that does not.

Many parrotfish mask their scent by sleeping in a mucus "sleeping bag."

Skunks

The first thing most people think of when they hear the word *skunk* is "horrible smell!"

Skunks defend themselves by spraying foul-smelling liquid. Luckily, they give several warnings first. If approached by a predator, skunks hiss and growl, stamp their feet, and lift their tails. If the predator does not leave, skunks blast it with a foul-smelling yellow liquid.

A Skunk's Smell

A skunk's liquid spray makes fur and clothing smell very bad. The smell can be very difficult to remove.

A skunk raises its tail to spray predators that will not leave it alone.

A beautiful stink bug can release a horrible smell if it feels threatened.

Stink Bugs

Stink bugs can really make a stink! They use their stink to defend themselves from predators.

Stink bugs release a smelly liquid when attacked or handled roughly. The liquid is released through openings between the first and second pair of legs. Not only does it stink, but it also irritates the skin and the eyes of the victim.

Vital Statistics

- **Length:** 0.2 to 2 in (5 to 50 millimeters)
- **Habitat:** plants
- **Distribution:** almost worldwide
- **Predators:** lizards and birds

A Stink Bug's Smell

A stink bug's smell stays on flowers and leaves and makes them taste disgusting.

Vital Statistics

- **Length with tail:** 6.6 ft (2 m)
- **Habitat:** all areas except tropical forests and arid deserts
- **Distribution:** Europe, Asia, and North America
- **Predators:** other wolves

A Gray Wolf's Hackles

The hairs that stand up on a gray wolf's neck and back are called hackles. A gray wolf with raised hackles is feeling aggressive or angry.

Gray Wolves

When gray wolves get angry, the hairs on their necks and backs stand up. They suddenly look much bigger to predators.

When gray wolves feel threatened by an intruder, they give several warning signs. The hairs along their backs stand straight up, and they stare at the intruder. Then they pull back their lips to reveal their teeth and they snarl menacingly. If the intruder does not back off, gray wolves attack.

A gray wolf raises its hackles to warn intruders to move away.

A long-eared owl makes itself look huge when it is defending itself from predators.

Vital Statistics

- **Length:** 1.1 to 1.2 ft (34 to 37 cm)
- **Habitat:** forest edges and woodlands
- **Distribution:** Africa, Europe, Asia, and North America
- **Predators:** owls, eagles, hawks, and buzzards

Long-eared Owls

When threatened, long-eared owls make themselves look two to three times larger than they really are.

A female long-eared owl makes herself look huge and scary when a predator approaches her nest. She spreads her wings out, lowers her head, and glares at the predator. If the predator does not leave, she attacks it with her razor-sharp **talons**.

A Long-eared Owl's Wings and Feathers

A long-eared owl makes itself look huge by spreading its wings and puffing up its feathers. It also defends its eggs or its young by giving alarm calls and snapping its beak.

23

An inflated porcupine fish does not look good to eat with its sharp, prickly spines.

Vital Statistics

- **Length:** up to 3 ft (91 cm)
- **Habitat:** shallow seas
- **Distribution:** almost worldwide
- **Predators:** tuna, sharks, dolphins, and whales

A Porcupine Fish's Body

A porcupine fish swallows lots of gulps of water to stretch its stomach. As its stomach stretches, the fish looks like a balloon blowing up.

Porcupine Fish

An **inflated** porcupine fish is an amazing sight. It looks more like a prickly beach ball than a fish.

Porcupine fish swallow water or air when they feel threatened. They swell up to two or three times their original size. This makes their sharp spines stick straight out. They become too round and prickly for a predator to bite into or swallow.

Common Chuckwallas

When common chuckwallas sense danger, they wedge themselves into rock crevices. Then they inflate their bodies with air so they cannot be dragged out.

Common chuckwallas are the second-largest lizards in the United States and they are very shy. If a common chuckwalla is approached, it races to nearby rocks and slips into a narrow crevice. It gulps air so that its body swells up and fills the crevice. Once it is wedged tightly, a predator cannot pull it out.

Vital Statistics

- **Length:** 1.3 ft (40 cm)
- **Habitat:** deserts with rocky hills
- **Distribution:** North America
- **Predators:** birds of prey and coyotes

A Common Chuckwalla's Body

A common chuckwalla has loose skin on the sides of its neck and body. Its skin becomes tighter when it swallows air.

A common chuckwalla crawls into a rock crevice and fills itself with air until it is tightly wedged.

A young broad-headed skink has a bright blue tail that it can shed to escape from predators.

Vital Statistics

- **Length:** 1.1 ft (33 cm)
- **Habitat:** damp forests
- **Distribution:** North America
- **Predators:** snakes

A Broad-headed Skink's Tail

A broad-headed skink can choose whether to shed all or part of its tail.

Broad-headed Skinks

Broad-headed skinks shed their tails when seized by predators. They leave their tails wriggling wildly on the ground. Then they grow new ones later.

A broad-headed skink has many defenses. Like most lizards, it has camouflaged skin. When threatened, it either stays very still or races away at top speed. If all other defenses fail, the broad-headed skink sheds its tail. It races away and hides while the predator is looking at the wriggling tail.

Sea Cucumbers

Some sea cucumbers have a neat trick to distract predators. They shoot sticky threads out of their bottoms!

Sea cucumbers do not look as if they can defend themselves, but they can. Some sea cucumbers shoot fine threads at attacking predators. The threads cover a predator like a sticky net. Some sea cucumbers can even shoot out their whole **digestive system**!

Vital Statistics

- **Length:** 0.8 in to 6.6 ft (2 cm to 2 m)
- **Habitat:** oceans
- **Distribution:** all oceans worldwide
- **Predators:** sea stars, crabs, fish, and turtles

A Sea Cucumber's Threads

A sea cucumber's threads become much longer and stickier after they are shot out. They stick all over a predator and stop it from moving.

Some sea cucumbers can defend themselves by firing white, sticky threads.

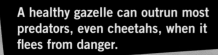

A healthy gazelle can outrun most predators, even cheetahs, when it flees from danger.

Vital Statistics

- **Height at shoulder:** 2 to 3 ft (60 to 90 cm)
- **Habitat:** grasslands and open plains
- **Distribution:** Africa and Asia
- **Predators:** cheetahs, leopards, lions, hunting dogs, and hyenas

A Gazelle's Fleeing Behavior

Some gazelles can run farther and turn faster than cheetahs, which are the fastest animals on land.

Gazelles

A gazelle's only defense is to flee from predators. A gazelle races away at top speed when it sees a predator getting ready to attack it.

Since they live in areas where they can be easily seen by predators, gazelles stay **alert**. Gazelles watch and listen for signs of danger as they nibble plants and leaves. When they are alarmed, they bounce up and down on stiff legs. Then they flee at speeds of up to 50 miles (80 kilometers) per hour.

Squids

Squids zoom through the water using jet **propulsion** when they need to make a speedy getaway.

Squids escape from predators by rocketing backward. They suck in water when they are under attack. Then they force the water out through a tube called a siphon. This makes them shoot backward at tremendous speed. Squids change direction by moving the siphon.

Vital Statistics

- **Length:** 0.8 in to 59 ft (2 cm to 18 m)
- **Habitat:** seas and oceans
- **Distribution:** almost worldwide
- **Predators:** tuna, sharks, seals, dolphins, and whales

A Squid's Fleeing Behavior

A squid goes faster by pushing water out through its siphon with greater force. Some squids go so fast that they shoot out of the water and onto the decks of passing boats!

Squids shoot backward using jet propulsion to flee from predators.

Double Defenses

Many animals have not just one, but two ways
to defend themselves from predators.

Tawny Frogmouths

Tawny frogmouths have excellent
defenses. They use tricky behavior
and camouflage to hide themselves
from predators.

A Tawny Frogmouth's Tricky Behavior

At the slightest hint of danger, a tawny
frogmouth freezes. It tucks in its
feathers, raises its beak, and closes its
eyes. It stays very still, looking just like
a broken branch.

A Tawny Frogmouth's Camouflage

A tawny frogmouth's color and patterns
help it to hide in trees. A tawny
frogmouth's feathers are gray and brown
with black streaks. They match tree bark
perfectly.

Glossary

alert	watching for signs of danger
deter	put off or discourage
digestive system	the parts of the body used for processing food
flocks	groups of animals that live and feed together
habitats	areas where animals live, feed, and breed
inflated	filled with air
jet propulsion	movement caused by water being forced out of the body
mask	cover or disguise
predators	animals that hunt and kill other animals for food
prey	animals that are hunted and caught for food by other animals
rely	depend
revealed	shown; made visible
scans	looks often over a big area
scent	smell
shed	removed or taken off
startle	frighten suddenly
talons	the sharp claws of a bird of prey
venomous	poisonous
writhe	twist the body; squirm

Index